The *Mystery* of *Humanity*

tranquility & survival

Molana Shah Maghsoud Sadegh Angha
"Pir Oveyssi"

Shahmaghsoudi (Angha) Heritage Series on Sufism

UNIVERSITY PRESS OF AMERICA, INC.
Lanham   New York   London

4720 Boston Way
Lanham, Maryland 20706

3 Henrietta Street
London, WC2E 8LU England

Library of Congress Cataloging-in-Publication Data

Sàdiq ' Anqā
(Essays. English. Selections)
The mystery of humanity : tranquility & survival / Sadegh Angha, "Pir
Oveyssi".
p.   cm. -- (Shahmaghsoudi (Angha) heritage series on Sufism)
Commentaries writted by Dr. W. Brown.
Includes bibliographical references.
Partial Contents: Nirvan--Message from the soul--Psalm of the gods.
1. Maktab Tarighe Oveyssi Shahmaghsoudi.   I. Brown, William R.
(William Richard). 1934- I. Title. III. Series.
BP189.7.M28S235   1995   297'.4--dc20   95-441128 CIP

ISBN 0-8191-9793-9 (Pbk: alk: ppr.)

Molana Shah Maghsoud Sadegh Angha
"Pir Oveyssi"

Contents

In translating from the Persian, the masculine gender is used in references to God and human being (*"ensan"*). This is partly for convenience but also because the Persian language has no distinct gender denominations; thus, the Persian pronoun *"ou"* may mean "he" as well as "she" with the proper meaning contextually determined.

In God's Great Name

"If the alphabet of the spiritual book

were revealed to man,

and the secrets of the book

of the soul discovered,

he would not need the words

in the silent books,

and would be close to the state

of Omniscience."

From Fetus to Paradise:
The Evolutionary States of Man
Hazrat Molana Mir Ghotbeddin Mohammad Angha

Editorial Foreword

*T*he *Mystery of Humanity*, which contains three texts: *Nirvan*, *Message from the Soul*, and *Psalm of the Gods*, brings to the modern reader the inner lore of mystical truth about man's creation, existence, and eternity — in other words, man's quest for tranquility and survival. This tradition, known as *irfan*, means cognition and acquaintance of God, not through reasoning and deduction, but through heart discovery and inward vision. *Irfan* has been known in the West as Sufism, a word which has been used to denote the philosophical and historical approach of man throughout the ages to understand the origins and the way of *irfan*, and the word Sufi has been used to mean the *arif*, or he who has attained the most exalted state of existence in practicing the principles set forth by *irfan*.

The author, Molana Shah Maghsoud Sadegh Angha, known as Professor Angha by his Western students, traces his lineage to Hazrat Oveys Gharani,[*] one of the Prophet Mohammad's followers who lived at the time of the Prophet himself. Ronald Grisell in his book *Sufism*, writes about the author and Maktab Tarighat Oveyssi Shahmaghsoudi *(School of Islamic Sufism)*, which the author headed for more than thirty years:

"These are the followers of Oveys Gharani. As historical sources show, Oveys Gharani was honored with being given the first and original Robe from the Prophet Mohammad; he is consequently thought of as the founder of the religion. (Salman Farsi, equally respected, is thought of as the co-founder). All the various branches of Sufism can thus be seen to trace back to him.

"Oveys Gharani was the son of Amer, and was born in Najd, in Yemen. He dedicated his entire life to asceticism and piety. Of medium height, he was so slender that he has been called 'Shaarani,' or 'hair' in Arabic, indicating metaphorically that he was 'thin as a hair.' He is said to have been a camel herdsman, earning a living for his old, blind mother by feeding camels in the pasture, where he would spend entire nights praying. Because of his duties to his mother, it is said that he never actually succeeded in visiting the Prophet Mohammad; but he had accepted Mohammad's religion in his innermost heart, and was a faithful follower.

"Mohammad is said to have faced Yemen at times (where Oveys lived), and to have said: 'A blessing blows in

[*]The conventional Arabic transliteration is Uways al-Qarani.

from Yemen'. People would ask him: 'Who lives in Yemen?,' and the Prophet would reply 'A man by the name of Oveys Gharani.' Just before his death, the Prophet called for Imam Ali and Omar (the second caliph of Islam), and said 'Take my Robe to Yemen and give it to a man named Oveys. He is a man of moderate height, and is slender (shaarani). There is a white mark on the palm of his hand and on his side. He has acted as mediator between three tribes and God.' (Mediation in Islam means to intercede between God and a soul wishing to approach God and to beg His acceptance). 'When you see him, give him my blessing, and ask him to pray for my followers and to mediate for them, for many of my followers will be accepted by God through the mediation of this man.'"

Jalaleddin Molavi Balkhi, known as Rumi, and Sheikh Attar, with whom the Western reader is familiar, have both their roots of instructions from Sheikh Najmeddin Kobra, one of the masters of the School of Islamic Sufism. The genealogy that follows gives a complete lineage of the School and its Masters.

The Great Pir (Master), Professor Angha was born in Tehran, Iran on February 4, 1916. After completing his schooling, he continued his education with advanced studies in law, philosophy, literature, mathematics, physics, and chemistry. He has also had extensive experience in relativity theory, astrophysics (he operated his own astronomical observatory in Karaj, near Tehran); nuclear physics, physical chemistry, biochemistry and the science of Iranian alchemy which is totally different from its Western versions. He was also taught the delicate discipline of *irfan* for over 30 years under the guidance of his father, Molana Mir Ghotbeddin Mohammad Angha, whom he succeeded as the *Pir* of the School.

Professor Angha lived on the cultural borderland between East and West where *irfan* has flourished. He was deeply versed in the profound traditions of intuitive knowledge represented by *irfan*. He also knew in depth the teaching of Western science and philosophy. Dr. E. Shata, Professor of Literature at Cairo University writes: "During many sessions I had with Professor Angha — and each meeting was protracted hours and hours — I never felt fatigue, because his extraordinary spiritual expansion and his boundless knowledge distinguished him very clearly. He opened vast passages of various specialties like a new world to me. His book, *Psalm of the Gods*, is a loud cry to invite all beings to free themselves from mundane attachments, which are the heavy burdens of sins on their shoulders." Dr. Yoshimichi Maeda, a Japanese biologist who met and conferred with Professor Angha on several occasions writes in the introduction to *Dawn*: "Considering the vastness of subjects and individual knowledge of one man, these questions may be raised: Who is an *arif*? How much does he know? What is the reality of religions? What sort of training does an *arif* have that enables him to be like the boundless sea?"

Professor Angha once said: "I am a Moslem and a religious man, and whatever I do or have done is for individuals all over the world, to make them acquainted with the real principles of *irfan* and religion, and not for the unfounded traditions nor imaginary beliefs of one individual or group of people. This is because the smallest profit which an understanding between *irfan* and science can give humanity is the discovery of the truth of life."

The Great Pir wrote his thoughts and philosophy on a number of disciplines in more than 150 books. His major published works in English are: *Manifestations of Thought, Dawn, Al-Rasa'el* and *The Hidden Angles of Life*. The latter, published by the Multidisciplinary Publications in 1975, was his response to sixteen questions of a technical nature, posed by the members of the International Multidisciplinary Research Association, whose members have a broad interest in science and philosophy, with the intention of finding solutions to specific problems facing humanity. As stated in the Preface to *The Hidden Angles of Life*: "Certain of the problems appear to be quite intractable at present — yet are of considerable importance to the improvement of mental and physical well-being, ecological harmony, and perhaps even to the continuation of human society on this planet. As solutions are urgently, if not desperately, needed, it was hoped that as a noted *arif*, Professor Angha would be able to give some guidance to professionals working in the physical and biological sciences. To many scientific colleagues, this may seem an odd approach to be taken by a scientist. Nevertheless, science progresses most rapidly by 'leaps' of insight, by intuition, and by discoveries which are made almost as if by accident."

His books of poetry in the grand Persian tradition of the *masnavi* are yet to be translated. However, four of his books, *Ghazaliat, The Traditional Medicine of Iran, Weights and Measures* (revealing the secrets of alchemy), and *Principles of Faghr & Sufism* will be available in English in the near future.

Nirvan, Message from the Soul, and *Psalm of the Gods* have been translated and published in Arabic, French, German, Italian, and Spanish.

The present *Pir* of the School, Hazrat Pir, Molana Salaheddin Ali Nader Shah Angha, succeeded his father, the Great Pir, in 1980, and currently resides in the United States. The School now has over 400,000 students worldwide, and regular classes and seminars on the sciences, arts, literature, philosophy, religion, encompassed by the discipline of *irfan* are held in many parts of the world including, Austria, Canada, Denmark, France, Germany, Great Britain, India, Iran, Spain, Sweden, Switzerland, Turkey and the United States.

Avideh Shashaani
MA - Education, MA - Islamic Sufism & Philosophy
30 September 1985 Washington, DC

Prophet Mohammad
Imam Ali
Hazrat Oveys Gharani*
Hazrat Salman Farsi
Hazrat Habib-ibn Salim Ra'i
Hazrat Soltan Ebrahim Adham
Hazrat Abu Ali Shaqiq al-Balkhi
Hazrat Sheikh Abu Torab Nakhshabi
Hazrat Sheikh Abi Amr al-Istakhri
Hazrat Abu Ja'far Hazza
Hazrat Sheikh Kabir Abu Abdollah Mohammad-ibn Khafif Shirazi
Hazrat Sheikh Hossein Akkar
Hazrat Sheikh Morshed Abu-Isshaq Shahriar Kazerouni
Hazrat Khatib Abolfath Abdolkarim
Hazrat Ali-ibn Hassan Basri
Hazrat Serajeddin Abolfath Mahmoud-ibn Mahmoudi Sabouni Beyzavi
Hazrat Sheikh Abu Abdollah Rouzbehan Baghli Shirazi
Hazrat Sheikh Najmeddin Tamat-al Kobra Khivaghi
Hazrat Sheikh Ali Lala Ghaznavi
Hazrat Sheikh Ahmad Zaker Jowzeghani
Hazrat Noureddin Abdolrahman Esfarayeni
Hazrat Sheikh Alaoddowleh Semnani
Hazrat Mahmoud Mazdaghani
Hazrat Amir Seyyed Ali Hamedani
Hazrat Sheikh Ahmad Khatlani
Hazrat Seyyed Mohammad Abdollah Ghatifi al-Hasavi Nourbakhsh
Hazrat Shah Ghassem Feyzbakhsh
Hazrat Hossein Abarghoui Janbakhsh
Hazrat Darvish Malek Ali Joveyni
Hazrat Darvish Ali Sodeyri
Hazrat Darvish Kamaleddin Sodeyri
Hazrat Darvish Mohammad Mozaheb Karandehi (Pir Palandouz)
Hazrat Mir Mohammad Mo'men Sodeyri Sabzevari
Hazrat Mir Mohammad Taghi Shahi Mashhadi
Hazrat Mir Mozaffar Ali
Hazrat Mir Mohammad Ali
Hazrat Seyyed Shamseddin Mohammad
Hazrat Seyyed Abdolvahab Naini
Hazrat Haj Mohammad Hassan Kouzekanani
Hazrat Agha Abdolghader Jahromi
Hazrat Jalaleddin Ali Mir Abolfazl Angha
Hazrat Mir Ghotbeddin Mohammad Angha
Hazrat Molana Shah Maghsoud Sadegh Angha
Hazrat Salaheddin Ali Nader Shah Angha

The conventional Arabic transliteration is Uways al-Qarani

Genealogy of Maktab Tarighat Oveyssi Shahmaghsoudi
(School of Islamic Sufism)®

Preface

In the Name of God

*W*hen studying physics and mathematics in the United States during the years 1965-1972, I was often invited to give lectures on Islam. On many occasions when I had the opportunity to discuss some of my ideas on Islamic beliefs, it occurred to me that I should write about Sufism in Islam in greater detail, for my American friends.

I had discussed the contents of three of my father's works with Dr. Brown, who was professor of philosophy at Southwest Missouri State University. These were *Nirvan, Message from the Soul*, and *Psalm of the Gods*. In a series of essays, Professor Brown studied these works, drawing comparisons with Plato and other Western, as well as Eastern, philosophers. My return to Iran delayed the publication of these essays, but they are now published in this volume, together with a translation of the original texts mentioned above.

Introduction

Short Comment on *Irfan* (Sufism)

*A*n understanding of *irfan* and, even more so, the experience of an understanding of *irfan* and, even more so, the experience of the reality of *irfan*, requires a great deal of thorough and disciplined study and practice. However, in order to assist the reader, a few words may be said about the essence of *irfan*.

The word *"irfan"* means cognition and acquaintance. Cognition and acquaintance in this sense mean cognizing God through heart-discovery and inward vision, rather than through reasoning and deduction. If, with an open and sincere mind, one considers the teachings of the *urafa'* (Sufis) and the results of their search for cognition, it will be apparent that they invite man to a truth which transcends time and place. That is to say, they show man the path that will lead him to discover the truth, a truth that will

free him from the bondage of his natural and physical existence and ultimately lead him to the cognition of his true
identity. Thus, the essence of the message of the *urafa'* is that
each man, through personal experience and inward discovery, is able to cognize and establish the truth of his own
being. As the Prophet Mohammad has said: "Whosoever
cognizes his true self has cognized God."

The *arif* believes that that which exists and is constant is truth. The philosopher, on the other hand, searches for truth in changes; but since changes have no perma-
nence or constancy, his perception cannot lead to the
truth.

Philosophical thought has been divided into two
main groups: The first believes that cognizing reality is
impossible, with the Sceptics and the Sophists belonging to
this group; the second believes that cognizing the truth
and reality is possible, and the Peripatetics, the Deduc-
tionists, the Platonics, and the believers in *irfan* are of this
group.

The Peripatetic believes that cognizing reality and
truth is possible only through logical reasoning, and matters that are proved by such reasoning are truths even
though they are not accepted by religious laws.

The Deductionist says that though cognizing and
acquainting reality is possible only through logical reasoning, however those truths that are approved by religious
laws are acceptable.

The Platonic is of the view that reasoning is obtained and based on sensory understanding. Since sensory understanding and perception cannot be counted on, cognition can be obtained only through self-discipline and purification; that is, in this case, there is no need for reasoning. By self-discipline and purification one can cognize the truth through one's heart and consciousness. Therefore, acquaintance, obtained through self-discipline and purification, is the one and only truth, whether or not it is accepted by religious laws.

The *arif* believes that cognition can be obtained through self-discipline, purification, concentration, and meditation, but only those truths that are accepted and approved by religious laws are real truths; otherwise they are but illusions.

In commentaries on the classics of Sufism, such as *Golshan-e Raz* of Shabestari, *Masnavi* of Rumi, and *Mosibat Nameh* of Attar, *irfan* has been expounded as follows: Cognizing God is obtained in two ways; first through reasoning, understanding, affect through effect, essence through quality, and reality through facts; this is the philosopher's cognition. Second, acquainting God is obtained through self-discipline and purification. This second way is that of the Prophets and *urafa'*. This kind of cognition is obtained only through loving, obeying, and worshipping God by all means, with the self, heart, and mind under the supervision of a master who will be introduced inwardly and secretly by God through the seeker's heart.

Unity of Existence (Monism)

Some philosophers do not believe in the unity of existence and divide existence into necessities and possibilities. Others believe that substances (possibilities) are independent units, are not related to each other, and have different results.

For example, burning is the result or effect of fire, and putting out a fire is the result of water. Therefore, the plurality of effects and bases are the reason for plurality of the results of effects.

The *urafa'* believe in the unity of existence; thus, for them existence is a unified reality, and the reality is infinite being, and there is nothing but Him. All essences, qualities, possibilities, reasoning, etc., are His manifestations and the appearance of these manifestations are taken for the truth.

Infinite existence cannot and should not be explained within the bounds of limitation; it is infinite. "Unto Allah belong the East and the West, and whichever way ye turn, there is Allah's Countenance. Lo! Allah is all-embracing, all knowing." *(Holy Qur'an 2:115).*

In order to bring us closer to cognizing reality, the *urafa'* use examples such as this: If you take mirrors of many shapes and sizes — large, small, convex, concave, and other shapes — the reflection of a single being will appear differently in each of the mirrors. Now, if a man looks in these mirrors he will see different reflections and may think that these reflections are of different beings. If he searches for the being which is the basis for all these different reflections, he will discover that there exists one being and one reality, and that all the reflections are the being's manifestation which he had mistakenly taken as reality.

God appears in six different directions; and directions and manifestations are Him.

Nonexistence is not, and eternal existence is. Everything is the reflected manifestation of the mirror of existence. God's existence is reflected in it and existence is manifested from it. Since God is unique and there is nothing but Him, every manifestation of possibilities and qualities is His manifestation. The phrase "nonexistence" is used to describe the opposite of existence until existence can be understood, otherwise existence has no beginning, no ending, and no limitation.

This beginning has no beginning and this ending has no ending, things are not Him and there is nothing but Him. All these different appearances which look like plurality are but the manifestations of Him.

Seyr-va-Soluk

To be able to reach the point where the seeker sees nothing but God, there are seven stages through which he must pass. These trials and seekings are known as *seyr-va-soluk*.

The state of natural strength and pleasure — natural strength and pleasure refer to eating, drinking, sleeping, etc.

The seeker must pass this stage and separate his human characteristics from behaviors which are recognizable in all animals and living plants. The seeker must discipline himself to partake of the minimum amount of food and other natural instincts and pleasures.

The state of self — in this stage the seeker should sever all dependence and start a quiet and solitary life. He must begin with the designated prayers, obey religious laws; and, through repentance, endeavor, and purification, reach the point where he can step outside this illusive world.

The state of heart — the word "heart" is used here to signify the return, or revolution and change, that occurs in the seeker's internal behavior. The heart is the place where the door to the hidden world will open up to the sincere seeker.

The state of soul — at this stage the seeker has already passed the state of heart which, in a way, is the path of connection between soul and self. The seeker is free from earthly attachments and sentiments, and reaches the stage of absolute spirituality.

The state of secret — at this stage the seeker reaches the point of cognition and from then on, everywhere he looks he sees nothing but God. Where hearts are glorified by the light of cognition, everyway they turn, they first see God.

The state of hidden — the seeker, at this stage, will see and hear God only. He will see himself dissolved (he will become lost) in God. In this condition the veil will be lifted and the truth about existence will appear.

The state of more hidden — the difference between this stage and the previous one (in which the seeker sees himself dissolving in God) is that, at this stage, the seeker is not aware of his dissolution. This is the stage at which he reaches the state of supreme being. *Irfan* is the last state of *seyr-va-soluk* and the perfect stage of cognition. It has been said that: "A Sufi is ashamed in both worlds," which means no one wants the Sufi but God, or the Sufi has nothing to represent in either worlds.

The renowned Sufi, Khajeh Abdollah Ansari has said: "*Irfan* cannot be obtained through scholastic education." Abu-Abdollah Khafif said: "The truth of *irfan* is the separation from possessing and the abandoning of stipulations." He also has said: "*Irfan* is like a sea and the truth is a ship on it."

The eight principles of *irfan* are:

Zikr	(to remember) — remembering God at all times.	
Fikr	(to think, meditate) — being in the state of wondering.	
Sahar	(to awaken) — awakening of soul and body.	
Jui'i	(to hunger) — having exterior hunger (mind) and interior hunger (heart) to obtain the truth and to persist in the search.	
Suamt	(to observe silence) — ceasing to think and talk about worthless things.	
Saum	(to fast) — fasting of body and mind.	

Khalvat   (to observe solitude) — praying in solitude,
               externally and internally.

Khidmat   (to serve) — dissolving in the truth of the mas-
               ter and dissolving in the truth of existence, God.

Nirvan, Message from the Soul, and *Psalm of the Gods,*
which are masterpieces of *irfan* writing, express the truth
about creation, cognition, and acquaintance on which the
messages of the Prophets are based.

Besides these essays, some published works of my
father concerning *irfan,* conveyed through different disciplines are:

Manifestations of Thought (Sufism - philosophy)

Chanteh - Realm of the Sufi (Sufism - poetry)

Seyr-e Khergheh (Sufism - Masters of the Oveyssi School)

Love and Fate (Sufism - answers to Maurice Maeterling)

Shahed va Mashhoud (Sufism - poetry)

Seyr-al-Saer va Teyr-al-Nader (Sufism - poetry / dedicated to me)

Serr-ol-Hajar (Sufism - alchemy)

Psalms of Truth (Sufism - poetry)

Golzar-e Omid (Sufism - poetry / science of letters and numbers)

Daneshmandan-e Zarrebini (Sufism - limitation of knowledge
               through scholarship)

Iron (Sufism - alchemy)

Epic of Existence (Sufism - poetry)

Owzan va Mizan (Sufism - alchemy)

Al-Rasa'el (Sufism - four treatises on religion)

Hidden Angles of Life (Sufism - science)
Divan Ghazaliat (Sufism - poetry)
The Traditional Medicine of Iran (Sufism - science)

Molana Shah Maghsoud Sadegh Angha, (my father), was born on the 15th of Bahman 1294, (Iranian Calendar), which is the 4th of February, 1916, in Tehran, Iran. He has a vast background in philosophy, literature, and science. He received a university education and was a devotee of his father Lord Mir Ghotbeddin Mohammad Angha for thirty years, under whose supervision he was taught. His school is called "Oveyssi"— Maktab Tarighat Oveyssi Shahmagh-soudi *(School of Islamic Sufism)* — whose instructors trace in a continuing chain back to the Prophet Mohammad (peace and blessings upon him), the Prophet of Islam, in the following way:

Molana Shah Maghsoud Sadegh Angha received the Precept from his father, Lord Mir Ghotbeddin Mohammad Angha, and he from his father, Lord Jalaleddin Ali Mir Abolfazl Angha, and he from four instructors, (a) from Agha Abdolghader Jahromi, in the School of Oveyssi, (b) from Zahir-ol-Islam Mir Eyneddin Hossein Dezfouli in the School of Zahabi, (c) from Agha Seyyed Hossein Ghoreyshi Ghazvini in the School of Zahabi, and (d) from Agha Mohammad Jasbi from the School of Nematollahi, and Agha Abdolghader Jahromi from Haj Mohammad Hassan Kouze-kanani, and he from Seyyed Abdolvahab Naini, and he from

Seyyed Shamseddin Mohammad, and he from Mir Mohammad Ali, and he from Mir Mozaffar Ali, and he from Mir
Mohammad Taghi Shahi Mashhadi, and he from Mir Mohammad Mo'men Sodeyri Sabzevari (Sheikh Bahai and Feyz
are his devotees), and he from Darvish Mohammad
Mozaheb Karandehi (Pir Palandouz), and he from Darvish
Kamaleddin Sodeyri, and he from Darvish Ali Sodeyri, and
he from Darvish Malek Ali Joveyni, and he from Hossein
Abarghoui Janbakhsh, and he from Shah Ghassem Feyz-
bakhsh, and he from the great master Seyyed Mohammad
Abdollah Ghatifi al-Hasavi Nourbakhsh, and he from Sheikh
Ahmad Khatlani, and he from Amir Seyyed Ali Hamedani,
and he from Mahmoud Mazdaghani, and he from Sheikh
Alaoddowleh Semnani (Khajoui Kermani and Sheikh
Mohammad Shah Farahi are his devotees), and he from
Noureddin Abdolrahman Esfarayeni, and he from Sheikh
Ahmad Zaker Jowzeghani, and he from Sheikh Ali Lala
Ghaznavi (nephew of Sana'i Ghaznavi), and he from Sheikh
(Vali Tarash) Najmeddin Tamat-al Kobra Khivaghi (Sheikh
Najmeddin has had many instructors such as Isma'il Ghasri
and Ammar but his great instructor was Sheikh Abu
Abdollah Rouzbehan Baghli Shirazi), and Sheikh Abu
Abdollah Rouzbehan Baghli Shirazi from Serajeddin
Abdolfath Mahmoud-ibn Mahmoudi Sabouni Beyzavi, and
he from Ali-ibn Hassan Basri, and he from Khatib Abolfath
Abdolkarim, and he from Sheikh Morshed Abu-Isshaq
Shahriar Kazerouni, and he from Sheikh Hossein Akkar, and

he from Sheikh Kabir Abu Abdollah Mohammad-ibn Khafif Shirazi and he from two instructors one Abu Mohammad Rowaym (devotee of Joneyd) and another Abu Ja'far Hazza, and Abu Ja'far Hazza from Sheikh Abi Amr al-Istakhri, and he from Sheikh Abu Torab Nakhshabi, and he from Abu Ali Shaqiq al-Balkhi, and he from Soltan Ebrahim Adham, and he from Habib-ibn Salim Ra'i, and he from two great instructors, Oveys Gharani and Salman Farsi, and these two were instructed directly by the Prophet Mohammad and Imam Hazrat Ali.

The Prophet Mohammad and Imam Ali have spoken with grace and respect about the latter two masters in words that have never been pronounced concerning any other. Oveys Gharani and Salman Farsi were the followers of the Imams.

At present, my father is the only master of this School. He has many pupils who are being educated under his supervision. This way of instruction is called Oveyssi. Many books have been published about the masters of this School, some of which have been translated into foreign languages.

Finally, I wish to inform the reader that on my advice *Nirvan* has been translated into Arabic by one of my father's students, Dr. Mahmoud Oveyssian.

In this short introduction I have tried to write about Sufism in Islam as simply and completely as possible, so when the reader begins to study these three masterpieces, he will have a clear mind and a basic understanding about the philosophy behind the *arif's* thought.

Salaheddin Ali Nader Shah Angha
16 Dey, 1351
6 January, 1973 Tehran, Iran

Three Commentaries

1. Nirvan

*T*he dedication of this work reveals something of its derivations from the literature of Iran and the gnostic tradition for those who might be interested in tracing the literary background and development of this work. The purpose of this introduction, however, is not to trace the development of this work in history or as literature, but to try and furnish the new reader with a key to understanding the work. If one will open one's mind and clear away the prejudices that have been building there about what ought and ought not to be included in a poem, these works can have a philosophical as well as a poetic impact. This work might be called an Eastern version of everyman. It is certainly that, but it is more than a mere echoing of something found in Western literature; it has its unique meaning. It will be difficult for Western readers to grasp that this is also intended as a story of mankind, of man. Not mankind after the Greek sense of an essence of humanity. It is more like the Christian sense of all men sharing in a common being in relation to God, a true oneness. Nirvan, the ostensible hero of the first poem is not really any particular man. Not only is he not modeled after any historical figure, but even in his own realm of literary reality, he is not meant to be an individual. He is that which transcends the individual: he is the reality of man. He is the soul of man in its temporal struggle and its eternal relief. It is man moving toward his real humanity by discovering the reality within.

Comparisons sometimes help in understanding the literature of different cultures and sometimes even the literature of our own. For whatever light it may shed on either: Nirvan has something of the direct and simple mythology of the Garden of Eden story in the book of Genesis. Both are directed to Man rather than to any particular man, and both speak of man's relation to God and the existence and discovery of good and evil. In the customary way of analyzing these things, this story is an allegory, but it is intended as an allegory which yields the truth. It is meant to be a statement of true reality fit into a narrative tale of events given as taking place in time and space. Yet in Nirvan, there is postulated a realm of meaning that transcends temporal reality.

In Nirvan, the transcendence is within man himself. The story of Nirvan is a vehicle to carry the philosophical point that man finds eternity within himself: that eternity is not something separate from man's being, it is a realizable part of him. One of the chief philosophical claims of Nirvan is that there is a level of reality within us that most of us do not realize because we scatter our energies in so many diverse directions. Desire and pleasure become stumbling blocks for this reason: they entangle us in the temporal reality. They make us think in cause-effect terms or in terms of separation and fragmented being. The error in our practical life is that we miss the greatest salvation and the error in our philosophical life is that we are caught up in the materialistic illusion.

The difficulty with the philosophical subtlety is not the only difficulty that the first-time reader will have with this work. It will not be easy for most to understand the significance of angels and demons, the modern sophisticated reader may turn away from such things without even bothering with any possible meaning, but a closer look will reveal a multi-dimensional psychology within the angels and demons of the story. Granted that the psychology is not of the post-Freudian or even pre-Freudian sort to be found in the Western tradition. There is, however, a cogent point about the nature of man to be gathered from the angels and demons. This cogent point is that desires and emotions that make up the bulk of our inner life are as angels or demons in leading us toward or away from our discovery of the true reality of eternity that lies within. We can find or lose this reality by which of the manifold promptings of "angels or demons" we follow.

Another point of difficulty which one may find in reading Nirvan is the doubtful chronology. Places and events seem to appear and disappear with no continuity or reason at all. The narrative seems confusing as a result of the confusing chronology, but I think the confusion will be reduced if one realizes that the time-sequence is of "moral time" rather than physical time. In entering into the world of Nirvan, the world of ordinary time is left behind. The determination of the occurrence of events is not their dramatic place or the narrative, but rather the significance of the acts to the realization of true reality. Thus, we are told that Nirvan is a saint until misled by demons. We are caught up in the narrative and extract a picture of a man being led off from his straight and narrow path by some hairy demons breathing a little fire. The picture means rather that we begin our journey in the path of purity. It is the present divinity within. But that purity is challenged from all sides: along come the temptations of the flesh or the world, perhaps in puberty. They seem to us good, but they are evil, disguised as good. They harbor within us the seed of delusion and loss of the divine. Thus, the fall of Nirvan is not a specific event in time, but a possibility we all face in many events in time. The only meaningful time in Nirvan is the moral sense of time. By "moral sense of time" I mean that time is only brought into the narrative when it means something to the venture of the soul — Nirvan. Time is a part of the false reality of separation. It arises from our mistaken belief in our own separate being, another delusion of the senses and desires.

At this point the moral landscape—but not the religious—begins to look like Plato, but there are differences. In Nirvan, as in much of Plato, the world is a dichotomy between Good and Evil, between the Real and the Phenomenal, between the Mind and the Senses. Further, in Nirvan the real is the eternal and time is only its moving image, as in Plato. These and other likenesses quickly lead one to believe that there is a common insight in the two philosophers. In both philosophers the essential view of man leads them to denigrate the role of the senses, the importance of the things of this world and it also leads them toward a vision of mystical transcendence as the salvation of man.

The chief difference between Nirvan and Plato is that they mirror a different religious tradition and culture in their writings. This difference manifests itself in the major role given to religion in Nirvan and the relatively minor role given to it by Plato. In Nirvan, man struggles between two kinds of potential within himself. The first is his temporal being: the desires, the senses, and separation. The second is his capability to reach something transcending the temporal: the eternal world. In this dimension — if it is reached by gnostic self-realization — man is no longer "a Man", he simply is "man", the true and eternal being that is the reality of all men. In our normal way of speaking, Man becomes men. Not that one man becomes many, but that he reaches the common humanity obscured by all illusions of the temporal. The philosophy of Nirvan will thus not fit into the platonic world of forms and particulars. In this world of Nirvan, there is an entirely different dimension of reality not included in Plato's metaphysical scheme: the reality of the particular becomes the universal. Although the metaphysical landscape is different, the moral perspective is not so different. Plato seemed all along to be looking for a way that the particular man at least could reach the universal. It was perhaps a consummation devoutly to be wished, a consummation which was not realized until the advent of neo-Platonism. In neo-Platonism, Western mysticism was born in the vision of a transcendence not at all unlike that of Nirvan.

To return to the meaning of Nirvan itself: the particular becoming universal is not the whole story by any means. The poem is an investigation of transcendence. This transcendent state is one where all illusions can be swept away and knowledge — a pure intuition — ascends to the center of the being. This is the reality of God which Nirvan discovers within himself, an obviously agnostic illusion. This is the Godhead of true gnostic salvation. Ontologically, man has transcended the illusory temporal world of the senses, in the claim of the poem. Man has also transcended the two worlds of the philosopher's distinction; he has attained gnostic eternity. This is the eternity, the infinity within. Nirvan is not a story of neo-Platonic salvation, but of a gnostic salvation: the transcendence is within. In the story itself, salvation is symbolized by the swan, "a majestic swan." This swan is the symbol for Christ and His salvation, but it is only a symbolic Christ, Christ as the one who found this Godhead within, most perfectly. The salvation of Nirvan is a somewhat easternized view of Christian salvation. It is the acceptance of Christ's model and of the reality of his divinity, but without the Christian tradition and ritual. Nirvan, as a person, represents the soul discovering the possibility of this salvation and the soul achieving the salvation. He is the epitome of the human soul. Thus, the whole story becomes an allegory, an allegory of the salvation of the soul. At the end of the story, Nirvan has attained his salvation. The story adds, in a literary touch, that Nirvan attained the Empyrean in the seventh day. This recalls the seven days of creation in the Old Testament. The seven days of creation become comparable to the seven days of salvation. As the world is made, so is man made, that is, so is the true man created out of the stumbling humanity. In this new world of the gnostics, man can overcome death and life. The path of life is now smooth. Nirvan ends on a somewhat parmenidean note:

"*Nonentity is not, and unique existence is.* Nirvan who had left the world of appearances, thrust away the dust, lost his identity and essence in the infinite and regained peace." Here ends the story, but here interpretation begins in earnest. These last phrases are philosophically some of the most difficult. In throwing off the dust of individuality, Nirvan begins to transcend what we so casually take as the "real" man in the mundane world. As far as the poem, Nirvan, is concerned, the real man is not in the mundane personality or activities of man at all. The reality of man is to be found in the transcendence, which takes man away from the illusions of the senses. All difference is discounted in the reality of Nirvan, in the world of Nirvan, there is no "real" world of time and space. Here there is no world of the narrative of events. The desert, the towns, and people of the senses have no reality, they merely appear, but they shadow a real world, a world eternal and created by the soul. Nirvan creates a world with the self-discovery, by the self-transcendence. But Nirvan is no particular person, Nirvan is the creative power of the soul.

2. Message from the Soul and Psalm of the Gods

This work takes the message of Nirvan out of the narrative form and into the aphoristic form of expression. The essential meaning or content of the Message is a statement of the great potential of man for good and evil. The mystical expression of the struggle of good and evil is somewhat reminiscent of the British poet William Blake, but the meaning is profoundly different. The struggle of good and evil in the Message is the struggle of the spiritual soul to overcome the carnal. It is also a clear statement about the present state of the world.

The sensuous soul has taken complete command in the ways of the world. The spiritual soul cannot find its freedom in the bondage to the vagaries of a carnally dominated world where war, greed, and rivalry control men's hearts. In Nirvan we saw how man wanders lost in the "Country of Oblivion", that is, in the wasteland of his own desires. The moral allegory in Nirvan is of the journey from desolation to salvation. The moral allegory is dropped in the *Message from the Soul* but the moral significance is the same. In place of the journey, *Message from the Soul* is a poem of the cosmos. It adumbrates a cosmology, a cosmology similar to that of Plato and some of the more mystical and less doctrinal Christian writers. In this cosmology, all the world of the senses, the objects, the desires, and rivalries are illusory. It is specifically the senses which delude the soul and make temporal (unreal) objects attractive to it. The transient temporal world is simply the production of the carnal soul under the influence of the senses. The world, as we call it and as we perceive it, is nothing more than a figment, literally a production of our weakness. The true reality, the one reality has none of the characteristics of the illusory world. To be a bit more systematic about it: What are the characteristics which are different?

First, the temporal world gives the illusion of the separation of men and the separation of the soul of man and God. This delusion of the temporal occurs because man in the maddened state of soul in his ordinary world has made himself something opposed to the rest of creation. He cannot find

God because he has deliberately separated himself from God. Thus does he erect churches and other institutions, such as science, in order to try and bring a semblance of order and oneness out of the chaos which he has made for himself. In *Message from the Soul*, the spiritual soul is really counseling the ordinary soul on how to escape the pitfalls of the illusory world. How is it possible? By giving up the claims of the sensuous soul. By a proper discipline of mind and senses, man can find his way away from the allurements of the life of separation. He can come to the realization of his own natural oneness with God, with the whole of the cosmos which he carries potentially within himself. The separation is the tortuous path in that all manner of devilish things must be pursued as if they were really what man were seeking. But, *Message from the Soul* tells us that man is really seeking immortality, and peace of mind. These things he really wants with his whole spiritual soul, but he allows himself to be deceived into creating a false desire for other unnecessary things.

The second difference between the two worlds in the view of Master Angha is that the world of the temporal is the world of death as the world of spiritual soul is the world of eternity. In defeating the sensuous soul and in coming to the realization of the unreality of that world, man moves closer to the divinity, the complete oneness in himself. He discovers the kingdom of heaven within. That kingdom is the immortality which man really seeks without realizing it. Man looks for immortality everywhere, in children, in creative acts and even in his miserable sensuous soul, but he can only truly find it by ceasing to look outside himself. The reality of eternity is within; it is there for everyman to discover, if he has the will and the courage. In realizing his own eternity within, man achieves it. When he finds the reality which does not depend upon the sensuous, he has attained it. Master Angha does not entirely condemn the senses, they are merely windows, but they become evil when we form our reality around them and take them as guides for the soul. They feed the carnal soul. It is the indulgence of the sensuous reality that is bad because it leads us away from the true reality.

The third difference is that the spiritual soul has true knowledge while the sensuous soul is deceived into thinking that its wanderings are knowledge. Master Angha's philosophy is gnostic. It is knowledge that is the lever of salvation, but his gnosticism is moderated by his belief that it is the heart — literally — which is the means of salvation. The spiritual soul is the agency of the heart, it is, metaphorically, the voice of the heart. The heart is the means to oneness which is synonymous with salvation.

The talk of two worlds and two souls, reminiscent of Plato, may mislead one. There is only one reality. This cosmology is entirely monistic. The one reality is open in many directions, but it in no sense is split or diverse. The *Message from the Soul* is a message of reality. As in Plato, this reality has what we call a moral dimension built in, reality is a value, it is good. The triumvirate of Greek philosophy can be completed in this philosophy. Truth as well as beauty and goodness reside in the one reality: all else is ugliness and falsity. The illusions delude in many directions: a split, a gap between body and soul, transience or temporality, all the desires of the carnal soul and not the least the whole babble of the contemporary world: all of these are summed up in the final illusion of death. As in Plato, *Message from the Soul* counsels us to welcome the death of the body, of all carnality, to move toward the oneness of eternity within.

This philosophy is not all cosmology or gnostic mysticism. There is a very practical and political side to it. There is a political message from the soul. The message follows from the vision of true reality and the awareness and hatred of illusion, but it makes a statement in its own right. The message is that in politics as in life itself, what makes for the realization of being in its positive manifestation is beautiful, what does not is ugly. Society becomes, rather inevitably is, a reflection of our souls. When people are slaves to the negative and seek to find themselves in desires, they like leaders and movements which will flatter their desires. Those men who do not understand the value of life will worship death in carnal transience.

All who are interested only in gain in the world become rebellious to the masters who could point them the right way to true life. They are slaves to their own desires, a slavery worse than the chains of legal bondage. In our age of turmoil, the virtues that bring men toward the realization of oneness have been thrown over for the vices that tear men apart. Tenderness in the body politic is killed and men become ready for any sort of rebellion that promises more material gain to them however others may suffer and however little they may approach what they really want: peace and immortality. Such men are dupes of the lies they choose to believe with others. They begin to believe that all they want is more material wealth, more illusion. The *Message from the Soul* says that the only way to true political reform and to ending the perpetual war and viciousness of men would be for men to begin to realize what it is that they really want and to forsake all substitutes. Only as man begins to penetrate the illusion of the sensuous in politics as in his own life will he begin to move toward the cosmological oneness which would end all possible political friction. Socially as well as personally we are part of the One. If we accomplish the victory over ourselves, the last victory, utopia, will be realizable because men will live to promote being. The true harmony between ruler and ruled will be achieved. The total reality will not be increased by this activity, it cannot be, but it will be actualized in a positive rather than in a negative way. The *Message from the Soul* is that man can find his way out of the illusion of his senses and desires. He thinks himself in need of those desires and the rebellions they engender, but one who clearly sees the treachery of the senses either as manifested to himself or in the lies of false prophets and leaders escapes the delusion. He knows that he does not need these things. The soul can find its way to truth, rid of lies and deceptions within itself and within its society. It can ascend to the good graces of the eternal. This is a message of salvation through intellect seeing through the false ways of the senses to turn the heart toward the true path of delight. A clear message, but unfortunately easier to give than to follow.

The last of the trilogy, *Psalm of the Gods*, is a statement of a vision. It has something of the flavor of the Book of Revelations, and the Beatitudes. It is a mixture of practical moral advice: "The wise man knows that he does not know and the fool does not"; and an apocalyptic vision of the final truth of existence: "Until dawn the holy messengers whispered the realistic visions of the Gods upon the sky of existence and gave power to the life of man." The poem is more than a vision of expression of practical morality. It is a statement of transcendence of the spirit, of the coming together of the divine and the human in purity. It is a religious vision in that sense as much or more than a moral vision. It is assuredly philosophical in its own way, a philosophical statement wrapped in the intense mystical and poetic vision of a religious experience.

The *Psalm of the Gods* has a mere suggestion of time in that it seems to take us back to a primordial time when all was joy and virtue and kindness. In this beginning there was perfection. But spirit slipped away from the oneness into incarnation and its purity was spotted by ugliness, triviality, and hate. The spirit's descent into life is not meant to be a particular event, however, it is rather a falling away from the eternal sphere of the real potential within us. The spirit descending into life begins to take on the impurity of the earth which fosters, like the second stage of the diffusion of oneness in the neo-platonic cosmology, the birth of thought. Throughout its incarnation, spirit looks longingly back, it knows of the purity of its original in the *Psalm of the Gods* as in the neo-platonic vision. In the *Psalm* also the moral goal is for spirit to once again ascend into the realm of purity. The process is one of return, return to a former state, ruined by the earth-dwelling of the spirit. But again this progression is not merely one of maturing in time; this is a vision which transcends time. The purity beckons in the future as in the past, but actually is in neither. Our perspective gives the temporal dimension, we happen upon it at one time or another and look upon it as past or as future, but in itself, there is nothing of time to affect it.

What may be said of time may also be said of purity itself. This purity is not a mere subjective state or a platonic idea. This purity is in fact intended to be a reality, a reality which exists even now and which can be discovered, if man but has the strength and the wisdom to uncover it. It is the purity of God and salvation. Throughout the *Psalm*, the ambiguity, the deep polarity of spirit in the flesh is brought out by the juxtaposition of visions of purity with visions of defeat of the spirit. These works are the expression of a philosophy naturally poetic, naturally religious, unashamedly mystical, unashamedly full of belief. There are no extended arguments to prove the points to weary readers. There is no attempt to convince one that this vision, these works, are the only legitimate philosophical system. The works are allowed to speak for themselves. In the talk of worms and sextons and angels and spirit there recurs the theme of God as manifesting himself in human existence, in the human heart. God is the focus of purity as He is the source. He is the alpha and the omega. Following the whole trilogy, we see the search of everyman for his own identity come to fulfillment in the vision of man completed in the awareness and striving toward the transcendent oneness that is God within. This introduction has tried to capture something of the essential purity and ingenuousness of the works themselves. It is understandable that with all its scepticism, Western philosophy might be wary of much of religious orthodoxy, but it also tends to shut out the wide range of experience, meaningful experience, which makes up the reality of man's search for God. To ignore the existential validity of the religious and spiritual life, leaves a philosophy superficial, feeding on the crumbs dropped from the full table of scientific inquiry. Master Angha's gnosticism is not the only expression of man's search for God. It does not give us any final answer to that search, which must always be individual, but it does look to those experiences which dare to look beyond the shallow worldliness and secularism and scientism of much modern thought. If these works help to turn anyone toward the inner life of the daring of faith, the joy of transcendence, and the reality of the mystical, they have undoubtedly succeeded.

3. Life's true purpose

Concentration of an individual's entire powers, homed at a heavenly point inside his heart, will acquaint him with his actual being, and assures him of being able to succeed in reaching happiness, an everlasting peace, and eternal life.

This is a rule, that in any learning process the following conditions are absolute necessities: a teacher in whose knowledge and identity no doubt exists and a student who is talented, receptive and who is devoted to the task of learning, must be present. In order to obtain the spiritual results in religions these conditions must also be met. The fact the prophets draw the attention of the people to holy personalities such as they, who come in the future to do the teaching, is the above point. The books *Psalms of Truth*, and *Golzar-e Omid, Shahed va Mashhood*, and *Seyr-al Saer va Teyr-al Nader* have been written with the clarification of this point in mind.

All efforts mankind uses, in whatever way or through whatever means, are really attempts to live in tranquility and remove death. Whatever instructions result in obtaining these two goals, directly, are to be respected and followed. The means that serve this purpose only temporarily will lead one into helplessness and death at some inopportune moment.

For a real man, life, in its true sense, with all its physical and spiritual conditions, is both the road and the destination. It is observed in the works of some philosophers that a portion of either the physical life or of the spiritual life is sacrificed in order to achieve perfection in the other part. This is not in accordance with the philosophy of true existence and neither does it accord with the place of man in his world. Because man's existence has become possible on both the physical and spiritual principles and conditions, the continuation of his life depends upon the omni-observance of true being.

The scientists follow their research through the study of the physical objects and their characteristics, through the perception of the senses. The theories of the philosophers of ethics become perfect by being based on the works of the prophets. In my idea, a school acting as a medium to fill the gap so as to acquaint the physical world with the vast world of the prophets is necessary in order for life to serve its true purpose. My efforts are to clarify the principles of such a school. The books *Chanteh — The Realm of the Sufi* and *Manifestations of Thought* try to pursue this goal.

It is my idea that the ethical philosophers, in order to be able to think correctly, would have to become acquainted properly in the principles of physics and cosmics of the world they live in. Otherwise they could not be positive of the correctness of their findings that they gain through thoughts they are unable to experience on the outside. If a thinker is unable to study and search through the world as he perceives it, the physical world as it exists and his true soul altogether at the same time, his findings will not be positive and realistic.

In the same manner that the brain does the thinking in relation to the outside world, the heart does it for the heavenly part. The reason the people are unaware of the powers of their hearts is because they are unfamiliar with heaven. I discovered that the heart in the body apart from its external and internal physiological relationships, also functions as a radar. Its weakness, disease, and stoppage is related to irregularities externally or internally. In any case, the heart is the channel for life and is what has formed the heaven of the prophets and the saints.

A principle set forth by Molana Shah Maghsoud Sadegh Angha is that, *"Words do not contain the meanings."*

Dr. W. R. Brown
Professor of Philosophy
Southwest Missouri State University

Note: These commentaries were written in 1972 by Dr. W. R. Brown, Professor of Philosophy at Southwest Missouri State University in Springfield, Missouri. They were intended as an introduction to the works and thought of the Great Pir, Molana Shah Maghsoud Sadegh Angha for English-speaking readers.

He is the Ever Alive, the Eternal

Calligraphy by the hand of
Molana Shah Maghsoud Sadegh Angha

In the Name
of the Merciful God

*P*raise be to God, who created man after His own image and illuminated the hearts of the learned with His own light.

Homage to the best of men, Mohammad, the Divine Messenger.

I, Sadegh, Son of Mir Ghotbeddin Mohammad, Son of Molana Jalaleddin Ali Abolfazl Oveyssi, known as "Angha," deeply meditated on the contents of the allegorical story *Ghorbat-e Gharbieh* by the Eminent Master, Sheikh Shahabeddin Sohrawardi. I found therein many deep and symbolic allusions.

Thus, seeking help from God, I decided to make an adaptation of the work under the title of *Nirvan*, in which I have tried to clarify the deeper esoteric implications of the original allegory.

Nirvan

*N*irvan lived a saint's life until he was misled by demons disguised as angels and lost the way of Truth, wherefrom he was cast out of the Vadi Imen and the Country of Ghods. He then found himself in a desolate land, east of the Vadi Imen. He said:

"Shortly after leaving our country, my envious companions put their diabolic plan into action. They threw off their deceptive masks, and, using a thousand pretexts, refused to accompany me, leaving me in the middle of the immense and hazardous desert. There I could find neither refuge, guide, or path. I was left in the hands of fate. As a rivulet flows down slopes and carries along any branch or brambles in its path, I walked ceaselessly on. I was engulfed in stifling and sinister dust clouds that rose as the wind swirled from the four corners of the infinite wilderness.

These dust clouds covered my being which were more transparent than magnetic rays, and slowly enveloped it in earthly covers." At that point Nirvan, like a bright star disappearing into the mouth of a frightful dragon, surrendered without resistance. He drifted into such a deep coma that he lost all memory of his land and previous life.

An emergent being, without name or origin, moved through a new existence, while the spirit of consciousness remained hidden in him. Time had not yet acquired its dimensions.

"In eternity, foot-prints are hardly recognizable. During that distant period of time or timelessness, after I had either been living in nonentity or had been forced to walk along the path of existence into being, I reached the isolated rocks, where I found my nature. I was locked in its fortress, wherefrom the smell of death arose; and from whose walls blood and poison dripped, the hunger of avidity, which saturated the human nature, tasted as a delicious nectar to the earthly host."

Eve, mother of all the living, took Nirvan to her bosom, to foster his source of life.

The celestial man, who had become his own tyrant, fell from the quiet paradise into the abyss of illusion, the Devil's Temple, and moving back and forth across the flames of torment and contradictory desires, began to mold this brutal existence, while his sins assailed him continuously.

The womb of perfidy inebriated the inhabitants of the Devil's Temple with the wine of impiety and transgression, and decorated the graves of the dead with gold, until they were deprived of the fruit of life.

Under this sky, ornamented by the light of stars, there is an abyss into which Satan has had the opportunity to carry the wicked, and in which the fire of Divine fury burns with great snapping flames, whence issue roars of ignorance. The bodies of sinners are torn to pieces and burn on contact, while remorse rises in their soul. This shall continue until the day on which the sun shall lose its splendor and the stars shall fall, and the seas shall overflow and the graves shall open. On that day, justice will come to each and everyone.

"A deep oblivion seized my soul; I no longer knew my name, and did not think of past happiness, nor did I regret it. I became another being, and my identity was lost beneath the colorful folds of nature, whose tissues were woven by Satan and, as a dark and dense cloud, I let myself be pulled into the frightful whirlwinds of my nature.

"A thick veil was drawn over my being, clouding the lucidity of my spirit. My true self was submerged, as if in a deep sleep. I could not recognize myself any longer, for I presented myself in many forms, but none of them was "I.'"

Textures of false beliefs and illusions dressed up the divine Nirvan in a mortuary-cloth, making him appear what he was not.

"Forced from the depth of my nature, I descended onto the abandoned land, the Country of Oblivion, as a man. I saw everything woven in gloomy colors, and wrapped in tangled yarns which gave it a strange aspect: I saw all this with the eyes of my nature, and by looking at it I became childishly happy."

Nirvan, full of desires, was driven into the Country of Oblivion, and the Abandoned land.

In this world, the principle of exchange governs all relations, an exchange conducted in a network set up by Satan, whereby hypocrisy and perfidy are constantly at war and peace. Angel-faced monsters, and hungry beasts, seemingly graceful, each bearing its own name, devour man; their success is fed by the blood of transgressors, and their deep darkness is a thick veil to the Light of Guidance.

These were the earthly companions of Nirvan, for the world of nature is a world of relativity, and relativity is the essential condition of existence in the Country of Oblivion.

The divine man, having passed through the rocky paths and winding passages of the Desert of Destiny, arrived at the Abandoned Land. He was so exhausted that he fell into a deep sleep. The infernal nightmares tortured him ceaselessly.

"I, Nirvan, was sleeping in the midst of all that dark and treacherous dust."

"One night, when the inhabitants of the Country of Oblivion, having forgotten their habits and customs, were sound asleep, and when the relativity of the world was lost in the darkness of human illusions, I heard the delightful songs of the inhabitants of the Vadi Imen, sifting through the prison of aspiration, and once again celestial hymns enraptured my soul.

"Nights pass and each sunrise gives birth to new hopes, but I was tied to my prison by the inexorable chains of material desires. The friendly voice prods the human soul to wage war with the enemies who repose beside him.

"I wanted to escape from the eyes of the Devil through the opening of my cell, taking as a guide the rays of hope, but the guardians of the Devil's Temple rose up to control my movements and surrounded me on all sides. Fear and hope sang the song of reunion in the depth of my being. The light beams of their new life passed over my being as light-footed angels."

Nirvan's regret grew immense, and his pain unbearable. He heard verses from the Book: "As a token of God and His Magnanimity did we not open thy heart unto thee? Have we not taken away the burdens that had bent thy back? We have made thy name famous; beside misfortune there is happiness. When the prayer is over, endure hardships, and turn toward thy Creator."

Real lovers are not diverted by the colors of the world; they are judged according to their patience. The refuge of Nirvan was his heart, messenger of the Country of Ghods.

The Father's messages awoke in Nirvan the echo of the forgotten language. As Nirvan began speaking in this language on the Abandoned Land, the natives, who were ignorant of that language, laughingly agreed that Nirvan had gone mad. They said: "He stares constantly and his speech is unintelligible. He does not enjoy life the way we do, and secludes himself, running away from even our shadows. He does not help society by kindling the fire of desires; he has turned his back to the customs of humanity, and loves death. To his taste, the delicious and exquisite foods of animal life are bitter and disagreeable."

Nirvan's story is an interesting one to hear. Some people who were burning in the flames of carnal desire, and who, because of the greediness of their associates, were deprived of the abundance of earthly pleasures, were trying to find refuge in death. But the death they were looking for was worse than the devilish life they were leading. They did not know that Nirvan's wealth was in his soul and his purity in his heart. The book "History of the World's Inhabitants" has two chapters. It starts with the love of the world and ends in the infinity of death. Their life is translated into these two phrases. Not the slightest sign of magnanimity and generosity can be found in them, and their aspirations are the vanguards of their death.

Nirvan found happiness in forsaking earthly pleasures. Until the attainment of complete salvation and eternal life, he will be bound to tear the clothes of death and cut the paths of life. He will kindle the fire of his heart by abstaining from worldly pleasures and meditating in solitude and sincerity.

In the Vadi Imen and the Country of Ghods, the laws of solitude prevail, and attachments, however delicate they may be, are but obstacles.

Whatever is fostered in the bosom of the earth is prey to the earth's belly. Wherever they may be, those who are remote from their country are infernal firebrands and their life is but the flame of Hell and their death nothing but the ashes of nonentity, even if they are disguised in the costumes of sincerity and chastity.

The colorful and disgraceful fences of the Devil's Temple strain Nirvan and torment him. In this human grave, he always thought of his previous covenants and remembered his native land, and wished to meet his people.

The flames of hell created by his ignorance, licked the lap of his aspiration and barred the way of his salvation. All day, until late into the night, the songs of stranger-friends chimed with ugly melodies, pleasing to the ears of the half-drunken prisoners of the Abandoned Land, enhancing pleasure and sin in the nature of those unfortunate beings who had lost their lives to aspirations.

An unknown fear and a devilish lust surrounded
Nirvan with their ugly and frightful forms and played before
his eyes the fire of the fight between life and death. Nirvan,
embarked on this Holy war as a courageous general who
hates and disdains defeat and eternal imprisonment, brushed
from his path all lust and aspiration, root and branch, as if
they were mere brambles.

One would say that the Devil was the creator and
master, and Nirvan his slave. This is an unjust and idiotic
idea cherished by the selfish and blood-thirsty transgressors
who have considered the rebellion of the weak against these
barbarous customs an unforgivable sin.

"I, Nirvan, will make every endeavor to liberate the
Truth from this grim prison of human nature. In this, I shall
not be deterred by any hardships. The end of the vicissitudes
and sufferings that I withstand at present will be peace, of
whose tranquility I have already had a foretaste in my existence." This freedom is not the one the earthly worshippers
talk about which consists of liberating a person from one
yoke in order to tie him to another bond of servitude. The
traps set by liars and the gifts offered by the messengers of
Satan cannot be a ransom for the divine Nirvan, because the
forces of darkness do not have enough depth to imprison the
divine light in their trembling bosom."

Nirvan, a native of the Vadi Imen, from the Country
of Ghods, says: "I was misled by sinners to the Abandoned
Land, and now I am secluded in the Devil's prison. The

ancient covenants and the peace I remember from the ancient fables have aroused in my soul a poignant nostalgia, and the hymn to my pains is: 'Oh, you angel of Truth and Sincerity, how could you let the flame of war, feud, and discord engulf Nirvan?' The thorns of the desert of oblivion have wounded my feet. 'Rise now to save your brothers and your kin whose hearts are dead. Nirvan, in the company of men, resembles a disintegrated body hidden in a grave. To him Thou hast blocked the ways of prayer, and his complaints are lost beneath the gloomy waves of his nature, and do not reach Thee. Winding paths form his way, and his faith, strong and solid, has been transformed into transient and poisoned beliefs."

"Open unto him his heart and consolidate his faith. Make his heart aware of his acts and let him be obedient, let his tongue be sincere, his ears disposed to listen, and his eyes prone to see.'

"The desire to live with my unenvious brothers who have risen to serve the Father saddens my heart, and the sorrow of separation heaves in my bosom. The flood of tears has stemmed the flow of my words. In the anxiety to hear my Father's voice, I become stupefied in the day time, and at night I sing burning songs of love all by myself.

"Is it not true that wild deer in immense plains find their watering place with Thy guidance? Is it not so that the perfume of flowers and spring blossoms are dispersed in infinity, just for the sake of reaching Thee? And are not the galaxies attracted by Thy will towards the emptiness of the void?

"'Call to Nirvan and forgive him his sins, so that he may be able to find the way to reach Thee. Nirvan is imprisoned by his own meanness, and the shame of his sins makes him blush. He curses the sinners' invitation. Return him, then, to the Country of Ghods and the Vadi Imen, with the help of the stars that always guide those who lose their way in the dark night; for the pain of separation has taken away the strength of his trembling knees.'"

Those who do not understand, look at Nirvan in astonishment. They ask themselves by what means Nirvan was deceived and led away from his land and his Father, whereas they themselves have been misled in the same manner, and prevented from serving the Father.

Nirvan's canticles enraptured the soul.

Driven wild by the dissidence of the Tree of Life, the Guardians of Mars raised their flags, lighted the sulphur and coated their arms with white deadly poison. Then they began the war, hoping that the coming peace may put an end to this confusing darkness. This war went on until, in token of the Luminous Temple, the sacred stone came out of the castle of vileness and began to lay the foundation of the house of worship for the pious.

The tower of human construction, built on six columns and as solid as lead, fell to ruin and was transformed into airy particles. Its columns cracked and its ruins became the dwelling of sharp-sighted, white-winged eagles.

Treasures of wisdom emerged from hiding and lay beside the seven stars, brighter than the moon, and passed the sign of the sun, and the ugliness of the five wandering planets disappeared. The walls of the Devil's fortress started to shake, their cracks were opened by the crashing forces of prayer, and its strong columns, which resembled imposing mountains, tumbled down like bundles of straw. Then Nirvan, at the Father's message and in reward for his patience in adversity, arose from the midst of disaster, passed through the deep darkness on the wings of the Messenger of Love, landed on the border of the Nile, and stared at its immense waves. The terrifying waves of the Nile menaced Nirvan and barred his way. This immense body of water, whose bottom is the foundation of Heaven, whose waves are the only horizon of the isolated, whose agitation is more frightful than a bloodthirsty dragon, and whose roars are worse than that of hungry beasts, resembles the altar where the disgraced were sacrificed: dark and filled with dead bodies.

After Nirvan had baptized his clothes in blood and thus had reached salvation, the spirit of redemption consolidated his paces on sea and earth, so that he could learn the words of the Book and board the ship of hope. Nirvan went up, reading the Book in his right hand, but not like those who are overwhelmed by their desire and who confound the sacred words with their natural impulses, and cup the blood of martyrs and saints and misconstrue the sacred words to hide their sins, until they arouse the spirit of anger against their own souls.

As a majestic swan, the Ship of Salvation slipped over the terrifying waves that crashed one after the other, and the child of Salvation saw in these waves the faces of the damned.

The roaring of the sea covered the laments of the drowned in their agony, and propagated their cries of torture, caused by the disintegration of the sinners' nerves.

Nirvan, accompanied by the canticles of the liberated Spirit, was led to Mount Sinai which was the highest of all mountains. Sirius remained static, darkness was split and the blinding light of the Tree of Life appeared, set aglow by the Salvation.

The ship, which had only been a vehicle of injustice, was destroyed. The sacrifices were ended. The graves opened and revealed the treasures they had hidden in their bosom. Thus Nirvan continued his voyage all alone, for a moment equal to thousands of years. Once in the skies more elevated than Nature, he tore away the curtain of clouds of the abyss of existence, thus attaining the end of shadows and hells.

It was then that the Truth appeared, and the beloved Child clothed in light, welcomed Nirvan and took him over the river overflowing with the blood of saints that waters the Tree of Life, barring the way to sinners and non-believers.

Then, the Word was revealed, the Absolute Truth appeared. A dazzling mirror, which had guided the pure, the innocent, and the redeemed, also shone before Nirvan. This beacon, which had one wick with three hundred and thirteen rays as the guardians of the twelve towers, was the Light of Guidance for Nirvan.

Nirvan was established.

Existence had neither peaks nor valleys. The dust of mutinies sank and death lost its significance. The balance of Justice measured Life.

On the seventh day, man was housed in the Empyrean. A sound of hope echoed in the infinite existence: "Nonentity is not, and unique Existence is." Nirvan who had left the world of appearances, thrust away the dust, lost his identity in the infinite, and regained peace.

Sadegh Angha
May 1960

Message
from the
Soul

Message from the Soul

*I*n my solitude, clear melodies of truth are tenderly in search of His visit and seek reunion with Him who is the strength and essence of all beauty.

Pity that my time is passing and to this moment is more than half gone. The warmth of my body is gradually turning cold and my eyes, grown weary, do not behold beauty as before. The flow of my love-filled songs in order to be prepared and offered to the circle of the inward looking seekers is becoming insincere.

Divine Protector, before the breath is choked in my throat, I beg of You to listen to the yearning of my heart and if it accords with Your wish, answer me and enhance the hope of my heart with Your blessings.

Before it is too late, may Your truthfulness descend tenderly into my breast, which is the place of tranquility, and bring joy to my expecting soul, for my time is passing relent-lessly. In those moments when, alone, I hurry to seek Him, the trail of my steps is hidden to the untrusted. When at the peak of love I lose myself in His radiance, I fully witness the vastness of His everlasting Oneness. The light in my heart is like a steady star in the deep clear sky whose image is reflect-ed at the bottom of a well, bright and radiant, and like Venus, the bride of the sky, calls gracefully to itself my entire being.

The inspiring sound of the Timeless Player makes my heart rejoice every new day, and my ear is faithful to its echoes. Even now I delight in hearing His melodies. This is my fate which has been ordained by His wisdom and pro-ceeds independently of my will.

O Divine Shepherd, the scattered herd of my senses and intellect have been under Your protection from the very time they took earthly life. I realized this many a time when, threatened by the carnal soul, my senses were protected by You, and not left in the darkness of night. Today, as my youthful energy is declining and my time running short, signs of painful old age begin to appear in my face and body: do not leave me unto myself. From the beginning I sowed the seeds of purity and truthfulness in my heart and soul at Your will, and now that the autumnal sun of my life is set-ting, help me harvest the crop of Your acceptance.

Weariness and fatigue are alien to the state of my heart, but they will vanish if You fill my heart with Your grace. The foundation of my body is shaking from lack of energy, and the vision of my eyes is gradually turning dark, and if deprived of the light of seeing You, I will wither in pain.

If in justice You choose to judge me by my deeds, it will be what my heart desires, and if in Your kindness You forgive my distressed soul, it will be Your mercy. All my deeds and intentions are for You. I am neither aware of what I do nor have I any knowledge of the path I have tread or will follow.

My capital is poverty and the gift of the poor to Your divine presence is unworthy. O Forgiving One, do not leave me unto myself, but guide me to the glory within, and touch me with Your supreme kindness.

O Eternity! How great and precious You are.

Realm of abundance and annihilation! How glorious and generous You are.

My soul rejoices because wholly I am entrusted to Your traditions and laws.

Greetings of my heart to the graceful, for like the morning breeze they pass on the path of purity, denying the temptations of their carnal soul.

My greetings to souls who at the peak of youth have sacredly beheld the warmth of love, and when the fire of the sun no longer burns, when the moon no longer shines, when the sky is no longer a scene of beauty, when the world ceases to tempt, and when souls no longer yearn, their hearts are filled with the wealth of awe in God.

The bounty of saplings depends upon the attention of the wise and attentive gardener, the safety of the flock on the guidance and protection of the alert shepherd, and the strength of hearts on association with the pure in heart. The best of the chosen is the altar of the heart, so consider carefully into what meadow you lead it and to whom you will entrust its training.

The delighted souls and the eyes that can see are in love with beauty, and their joy lies not in living in seclusion or living in the deep corners of sorrow.

The message from the soul is a divine inspiration. The essence of my heart is of truth, howsoever you may hear it! The humble soul hears the melody of the heavens and beholds the dominions of God. The divine message is heard on the horizons of equilibrium.

Nothing new takes place in the old land. Have you not known that the words and the verses and the laws of God are immortal?

All forms of life are at His command, and equilibrium and balance are His laws.

The wisdom that has been baptized through bondage and faith to God is a counsel worth knowing.

The breeze of the dawn of love, the freshness of the heavens, and the brightness of the shining stars are the places where the poor and humble wander. Doubts are what keep true happenings out of sight. Add to the tenderness of your soul for the truth to reveal itself and rejoice your soul.

The lights of truth shine through to the hearts, but hearts are too beset with transient temptations and desires.

Man insists on going astray and rebelling and is not afraid of the aimless wandering of his soul, but birds fear of being caught in nets and beasts are wary of traps.

A god that is worshipped for the sake of worldly fulfillment is not great.

Desire is a natural tendency in life, but pursuing it distances you farther from life.

The purification of dirty water is allowing water that is pure and clear to be separated from contaminants. Remaining attached to desires is like water that remains contaminated.

The flow of life is like a stream contaminated with desires; so in which part should we then search for the truth of life?

The eyes see, the nose smells, the taste-buds taste, the ears hear, and the fingers feel roughness, and softness, warmth and cold. Senses are for feeling and contact with nature. Mistakes made by them will not be questioned, their task is to feel the outside of things; their pleasure is the unknown states of the nervous system. We will not acquire the true knowledge of life through any findings resulting from the transactions of our sensory organs; the transient faces of nature and their different states are the short-lived, shallow, ripples of the sea of life. Remaining attached to them is painful, and parting from them is what brings peace and happiness.

Treachery of the senses and the nerves and their natural tendencies is a false shadow of the real you, an unrealistic existence which you refer to as "I", and in this false state of recognition you remain until your death. Breaking away from this delusion is the beginning of your coming upon yourself, and finding the truth of "I" in tranquility and freedom.

Individuation in existence is baseless, and segregation for the sake of self-praise is separation from the infinite; the way of such an individual is fraught with mistakes and errors, and leads to certain death.

It is gnosis that shall free you from all attachments, and strengthen your steps towards heaven and the true self until the time when you begin to live the new and real life. The gnostic does not take pride in earthly means and does not use them to help him move along the highway of life. He keeps watch over the self, holds time precious, and retains his concentration until the dawning of the sun of life, which is the source of tranquility of the soul.

Concentrate your thoughts in order not to perish in your earthly desires. Living in the world of transience leads to death; whatever is transient has descended from true life. Do not hang on to the pieces of wood drawn by the waves in the stormy sea of life, for they will not save you. Make the best of what has been given you. Overdoing and underdoing are two ways that lead to injustice, mortality, and instability.

Tenderness and harshness are distanced from each other; whatever appears to you as the reality of "self" is but one stage along that distance, and a signpost for search and recognition of the truth of life, the manifestation of death, as well as eternity and annihilation, the absolute and the conditional. The truth of "I" is totally unconditional; that is how it is infinite and eternal.

As for the true self, he is rich and needless, for his is the nature of all needs and he has no wish. He is eternal and everlasting, and annihilation is not a quality of his. He is steadfast and not unstable. Although the results of good and evil are attributed to him, by himself he is neither good nor bad. Study yourself, the thing that attracts you the most is what possesses you. In death you will be attracted by the same, and your world will be as such.

The divine vision is the observer of the shadows of life and, like a glistening star, bright and still, shines in your heart without hesitation. Concentrate your thoughts at this point in your heart and calm them; when it becomes steady and undisturbed the truth of your life will be revealed. If your thoughts turn to insignificant matters and blindly become a slave of your senses, your heart will disobey the commandments of God and will fail you along the rough road of life.

Guidance is in the union of thoughts, the heart, the senses, and nature; and going astray is disarray and confusion among these four.

Gather all your energies and concentrate them on *the source of life* in your heart for your findings to become imperishable, so that you will live in balance and tranquility and know eternity.

The gnostic sees his true self as he does his face in a mirror. The truthful observes his true self as he sees his face in the ripples of a stream. The lost does not see and will not see. He lives in a state of unawareness and foolishness. So shed the darkness of unawareness and foolishness which veil the light of truth. Enlighten the channel that extends from your heart to your brain and do not allow the heart and the brain to live apart, like two unfriendly neighbors unaware of each other.

To become eternal, dissipate any desire that tends to grow in your heart through the union of your heart and brain.

When all the combined energies of your senses together reach your heart and have no tendency to leave, you will find yourself. And because you will be nourished from *the source of life in your heart*, you will see your enlightened soul. Every bird flies back to its nest at nightfall and there finds comfort. So you, too, gather all the strength that is spread in your senses and body, concentrate and calm them in your heart at night, and manifest your luminous figure. If life is given to you by *the source of life in your heart*, you will not be subject to death.

For man continuously creates illusions that later are shattered; he creates these illusions but is not created by them. The rule and the will of God, his creations and works in existence, appear in the same manner. The eternal essence is manifested in the depths and surfaces of all that exists and will not vanish. But the unstable always comes together and later falls apart, while nothing is added to or taken away from existence. The birth of things is from the power of *the source of life* which is the creating angel of God; hence the birth of things is not for the purpose of increasing or decreasing existence. This infinite diffusion, from a part or the whole, the atom or the universe, brings forth constant births that sink into dispersion and death. The appearance of life is a presentation of this great diffusion and gathering, and the truth and the essence of life are eternal and immortal.

There are one hundred and one channels, starting from *the source of life in the heart* that through seventy one thousand lines irrigate the ten billion brain cells, so that the creation of God in this diffusion and gathering is brought to perfection. The source of life resides on the border between the heavens and the earth, and serves the will of God. At the point where the consciousness of life and the sleep of death confront each other, the first longs for eternity and the latter is attracted towards transience.

Search for truth in your heavenly double, at a third point in the heart, the point of union of the two worlds, one delicate and one harsh, between sleep and wakefulness. *The source of life in the heart* is the light of knowledge and certainty, and the very knowledge itself. And because it is all knowing, it is the source of all appearances and possibilities. It is the essence and the body of all things. Everything is brought to perfection by it. Present Him with nothing but poverty, for He is the source of all wealth. The names of God (the source of life which shines in the heart like a star) are read to hearts in truth, but the unwise hold sacred ceremonies and traditions whose meaning they do not know. The gnostics are the dear ones in heaven, for they keep the bowl of desires completely empty. For this reason, the secrets of God are found with them. Do not leave the land of your heart bare and fruitless like the desert, because it will not find its direction to truth.

Rough tracks overgrown with thorns will block the steps, and hearts entangled in desires will die at the foot of the idols they themselves have erected.

The bow whose arrow does not seek truth will break because of imbalance; but the arrow that is pulled with truthful intention will not go astray.

No kingdom will be safe while thieves and highway-robbers roam free. Bring the attention of your senses, the strength of your body, and your thoughts under the command of God, so that they will not be able to disobey, loot, or be treacherous.

Man is surrounded by his desires and actions, and leaving behind this world of tumult needs a firm and steadfast step.

The lie knows not truth; wickedness knows not grace; and cruelty knows not justice.

The deep corruptions of our time have insidiously cut off the ties of tenderness, softness, and righteousness from the heart.

The hypocrites do not bear fruit from the seed of the will of God. Their farms bear fruit from the seeds of sin and stubbornness and their hearts are disintegrated and pledged to idolatry.

The lie that has infested your greedy soul is like a disease that invades the body, and whatever food reaches it, is spoiled by this disease, which is thereby strengthened.

The greatest misfortune would be for the pains of childbirth to end with the death of the unborn child, and no child to be left to virtue.

Today your righteousness and well-being have turned to sin and ignorance, corrupt forces have engulfed you and have suffocated your soul because of your own injustice. Because your seeds have not been sown with justice your harvest will not be bountiful.

Because you have been left to your sins, if any among you prophesies to adultery, usury, obscenity, or injustice, you will accept his prophecy, for he will have preached according to your very desires.

This is because you are ruled by the senses and feelings. As with a group of traitors, they have stopped you from receiving blessings which are nurtured by God's protection. What hope for life and eternity will there be left for you?

Men, originally meant to be attracted to and absorbed in God with powers of love and justice, are now surrounded by deceit because of their transient desires and mistakes and ungratefulness, and have no savior.

Liars have chosen the lie and are wary of the truth. Hearts nourished from desires will be treacherous.

In the old days people would set their idols in temples and worship them. Today you have filled your hearts, which are the temples of God, with idols of desires, foolishness, ignorance, and darkness, and you worship them and turn to them for help. You have employed God in order to glorify your idols, until such time that the hand of God drags out your idols and destroys them. That will be a bad hour because your masters and rulers will be beheaded in disgrace and nothing will be left for you but sorrow and pain.

Why do you avoid the truthful and regard him as an enemy?

No farmer will block the wells and the springs of his farm, for what crops can be had from unharvested land? You have forgotten the kingdom and the justice of God and take pride in wicked acts and foolish thoughts.

Rebellion and stubbornness have put deep roots in your hearts, and have suffocated the saplings of honesty and truth, and turned your house of happiness and tranquility into a house of grief.

Do you ever, in times of hardship, wonder who and where your savior is, and whence the light of God shines for you?

Look at the times our fathers have left behind and do not follow the path of injustice and false promises.

The load of our trials is now heavier than before, and the endurance and patience of our hearts for truth much lighter.

Do not sell the jewels of your heart in return for fake coins. Do not put your inheritance of God at the feet of your desires. What hope is there for safety for he who is sinking helplessly in the middle of the swamp or quicksand?

Since you have cut the fruit of knowledge and severed the roots of truth from your hearts, I challenge you and declare that on the day of judgment the strength of the powerful, the wit of the thinkers, and the recklessness of the brave will not help, and everyone will be anxious about the results of his deeds. Only the pure and the humble will be saved.

The short-lived pleasures of a heart that finds its strength in harming the poor and heaping injustice upon the helpless are the flames of torment.

Do not rebel so much that you be abandoned on earth because of your sins; the lives of your children may yet be your redemption.

You oppress the poor for gain but do not put it to any use. Who has given you the assurance that you will survive to harvest what you sow?

Your savings are your sins, and you call your children to such deeds. Unrighteousness, treachery, and bribery cannot endure where there is justice.

Your continuous dissidence keeps the wise silent.

You make yourself appear as one of the pure, and observe rituals and ceremonies in the cloak of pride while stubbornness and corruption rule your heart. Your solitary companion is the devil on the inside and cruelty on the outside. Yet you will not believe that your palace of injustice will be overturned, and that the children will not rise up against you. The deeds of those who represent truth as untruth, innocence as evil, and God's oneness as duality, are the tricks of the devil and their intentions the orders of their evil souls. If the evil knew the way of truth, the words of God would emerge from his deeds and words, but since it is not so, only sinners are stable in the pursuit of desires.

The greedy fool prides himself in becoming bountiful and protected with effort that is baseless. Since justice will come in its time, sinners have been left to their sins, and the pure and wise to the tests of God. The wicked favor any rule that corrupts the soul and misleads humanity. Avoid the ways of the mean-hearted as they are nourished by unchastity, bribery, usury, confusion, and have allowed their desires to open the doors of treachery.

Time is the veil of events and container of circumstances.

Man's state of existence is the record of his deeds and the building stone of his life after death that knowingly or unknowingly he follows.

The heart is the source and the end of either corruption or goodness. Man is constantly in a state of movement and no one has a stable and tranquil place in the world to return to for peace. Experiences and trials are the stages through which your life passes; then what is your wish? After all these wanderings is it homelessness or tranquility that you seek? If you are in search of peace, then do not add to your wickedness in this endeavor.

The wicked try to purify themselves after every misdeed with false reasons, deluding their unhealthy hearts, and pretending to be just and pure, while the nourishment of their mouth, stomach, brain, and soul is impure with treachery and their seed will not be cleansed for seven and maybe up to seventy generations.

A merchant whose capital is purity and who transacts in truth with knowledge, and whose profit is closeness to God, is the servant of God.

The awakening of hearts is in the harmony of the soul with the truth of existence at the point of equilibrium. If six conditions come together with another six in your deeds, the sign of leadership will appear in you.

The six conditions are: concentration of thoughts; awareness of conscience; endurance and patience in reaching God; keeping of vows and firmness of step; finding complete trust in God; and clear sightedness. The six complementary deeds are: purifying the self; contemplating in solitude; endeavoring to discover the truth; concentrating the external and internal powers; being consistent in ascending the states; and attaining tranquility. When the heart of a disciple attends altogether to these twelve principles, his self and tongue will be safe from misdeeds.

Rejoice in the divine soul when it is present in your heart. Look deeply into the dreams of the truthful, who are the signs of guidance. Look for the signs of the heart so that the heavens will open to you, until your heart rises in the name of God and finds the happiness of justice.

Do not look upon the men of God with disbelief or lack of confidence, but look upon them with a pure heart. Learn from them the ways of destroying the framework of your false selves and pass through the gate of transformation and Divine birth. Experience the words of the men of God in the center of your heart, and become acquainted and know the truth of life that is the path of your existence.

If, in your faulty judgment, you do not rejoice in the truth of life, then death is definitely of pain and sorrow.

A true disciple watches with care the course he follows and has full knowledge of it; his concentration and inner silence, and his purity and awe of God are based on cognition and knowledge.

The high palaces of the wise are indeed elevated and no rebel can find his way to them.

Graft the sapling of your heart to *the source of life* so that it shall be nourished, until the blessed tree of justice bears fruit and permeates your being.

Unless the heart is roused in the name of God, the way of purification and union will be closed.

Ignorance and wickedness are the inheritors of blasphemy, just as famine and plague are the legacy of drought and war.

The enlightened souls rise in the name of God; and after total devastation, the ruins are rebuilt by their hands. This is the promise of my God who has ordered to justice. The divine message — the message that comes from the depths of the heavens guides the lost seekers to the house of truth, and the hand that heals with the power of God, and the soul that establishes and calms the surrendered hearts for them to live on — is vouchsaved by the Almighty God.

He who is guided will not be fooled by the ruse of the diabolical self, and the misled will not heed the call of God to be saved.

When God's justice is the ruler of fate, the stubbornness of the wicked, the wit of the learned, and the recklessness of the brave cannot pull a thorn from the foot or clear a stone from the road.

The poor who has inwardly witnessed and discovered his home in heaven will not be moved by the problems of earthly life; and the burdens and pressures of such life, as well as its pleasures, will not make his soul lose hope in receiving the blessings of God.

For the light of heaven always removes fear and sorrow from the sacred souls.

Time is short and the day of judgment is near.

Sadegh Angha
March 1968

Psalm
of the
Gods

Psalm of the Gods

A being of God's creation Sadegh, son of Lord Mir Ghotbeddin Mohammad, son of Lord Djalaleddin Ali Mir Abolfazl Angha, has recalled a realistic vision of an era of truth and purity, and silently repeats its incident:

In bygone ages when men were clear of heart and pure of soul,

When their hearts were the source of joy,

Life's melodies sprung from the love of the Gods,

And righteousness their existence ruled,

Ugliness had no place in their souls,

Virtue and kindness guided their deeds,

And holy was the security of the spirit in the realm of the heart.

Death a lesser shadow cast upon the tree of life, and souls the ways of the devil knew not,

Stagnant and stable were the dusts of imagination upon the earth,

And heavenly light filled creation,

And brimming with love and affection, hearts in tranquility waited with the dead of night, even the early dawn,

The silhouette of an angel, incarnation of truth, sent by God and dwelling in perfect harmony with the nature of man, appeared upon the steps of existence in the temple of the skies whispering the Psalm of the Gods calmly, in perfect tenderness, soothing to the eager ears of the Sons of Man.

⁂

These were his songs:

God encompasses the souls, and existence is the manifestation of His words.

The endeavors of the impure, the righteousness of the pure, all deeds and thoughts — nothing is concealed from the scope of His vision.

In the holy dignity of the Gods the hidden secrets are revealed, righteousness is praised, evil is nullified.

In life, the state of the dead counts for naught. The ignorant lay the foundations of their graves and tarnish the blessings with evil.

Man's soul in disharmony with earthly life has turned rebellious; for earth cultivates not evil and ugliness; rebellion and desire at the same instant as man, were born. Huddled together in existence are the wicked for they fear the legacy of their deeds.

But in simplicity do the poor live, nourished by the blessings of existence. In their own time they live and their crops they harvest not before it's time.

As the low, barren grass hides water that flows beneath the earth, so the impure's desires conceal the passage of his life, desires ever unfulfilled, and drinking from the cup of death, he weeps and is cast out.

The grave-digger earns his keep digging graves; the life of the greedy is none better.

To be left at the mercy of his sins, and to be resurrected in time for them, is man's greatest terror and torture.

The covetous and avaricious is but a greedy child, full of envy for the food on his neighbor's table.

Offense and crime are progenitors of the penal code, so the wishes of the greedy represent their baseness and incompetence.

⁂

The sinner's inner torment springs from remorse, in witness of his ugly deeds.

Crudely carved statues by idol-makers in the image of their desires gratify not, but arouse derision of the wise.

Pursuers of desires within their hearts cannot live, just as man cannot dwell in the same house with a rotting corpse.

The laws of the corrupt smooth the paths of the coward, providing pleasure for the greedy at the expense of the simple in heart and the ignorant; personal fancies and baseless traditions are these laws' foundations; yet however alluring their philosophy, it is but a veil upon the face of the truth of humanity.

Outdated ideas are a fertile soil for the propagation of superstition and transgression, shading the rights of humanity. Real man follows not traditions blindly, but hides purity and wisdom within his heart, living in complete simplicity.

The soul's innate manifestations are the messengers of man's existence.

All that serves corruption, destruction, and instability will in turn serve anger, greed, fear, hopelessness, senility, sickness, sorrow and death. And these are death's companions, born when man was born.

The heavens' knowledge never will be revealed by protecting or harming those fostered by the earth.

Poetic phrases, propagated by the philosophy of the age, are as illusions created by man's imagination about the soul.

Obstinacy and negligence are ways that man has learned from the book of individuation. Hence eternity's meaning to the lost is incomprehensible.

❖❖❖

The hearts of the heavenly angels are saturated with hope and tranquility.

In nature's destination the pacts of man are apparent, but to the senses they are unknown.

The profound secret of existence is discovered in the union of the seen and the hidden, thus is man acquainted with eternity's law.

Man's temporary attachments, at their zenith, ever conceal heavenly events from his sight.

Desires cause the eye of the heart to be blind and decorate ignorance for the perception of the human eye.

Useless is thought not meant for inner peace and tranquility, and worthless is knowledge that enhances not the personality.

The embryos of immature thoughts and incomplete wisdom are dead before they are born.

Real man is only he who keeps his living personality far from the fanciful motives of humanity.

❖

The blessed ones receive the truth of life without learning the rites and traditions of nations.

The waters of springs rise from the heart of the earth, flow through the cracks in the rocks, and their course is not obstructed by sediment or mud.

The Divine Souls expel strangers from their midst and allow them not to become obstinate, for the dignity of God accepts not any law other than peace and tranquility, and anxiety has nowhere to flourish.

The delicate have greater endurance than the harsh; thus strength lies in tranquility and not in worry and anxiety. The storm of the waters is of greater intensity at the shores than at the ocean depths.

The tranquil heart of the true man has far more splendor than the anxious mind of the sinner.

The Gods cast a shadow like the clouds and bring forth rain, and their fruit is the increase of the blessings upon the accepting earth.

The highlands refuse the waters but the valleys will be filled with them, creating trees, fruit, and fish; thus, the rebels are not admonished by the fallen.

The patience of the meek at times of tragedy is that which suppresses hypocrisy and selfishness.

The trees manifest their fruits from the knots of their branches, swords are used whilst naked, and heroes attain victory in defeat.

⁂

The ways of life have simple, yet complicated paths.

The Psalm of the Gods echo upon the graves.

Unfulfilled souls mistake their creations for the truths of life.

He who hears the Psalm of the Gods finds the way of life.

The melody of the angels enhances the delicacy of souls; and the tired, upon hearing them, find rest.

Those aware of their poverty shall receive wealth.

And those aware of their loss shall seek and find.

Broken teeth and infirm temperaments benefit not from food, and passions will not reach the height of tenderness.

Roots which penetrate in dry and stony ground receive no nourishment.

The messengers of time shall deliver the letter of life rapidly with love, and without delay, but man ignorantly stands upon a mount of dust and thinks there he will remain until eternity.

The wise knows that he does not know and the foolish does not.

The wild beast, when old and broken, suffers from lack of power, incapacity, and the weakness of its limbs.

⁂

In the existence of the wise there is no instability. The true man is the sky and earth that in balance live. Patient he is in times of calamity and at times of happiness virtuous, shattering the pillars of illusion which, like ancient temples, are filled with idols, and exposing the truth of his self for worship.

Man lives alone, and along the path of life a stranger is he to all, even to the moments of his own life. In this journey without return, the sorrow of desires will wither the freshness of his face and he takes steps towards the unknown, pledged between his past and future, straining for the lost songs long hidden in his own soul; and strange it is that before he finds them, he dies.

The existence of the ignorant and insane is pitiful and sad; it is as dry, lifeless leaves blown about aimlessly by the wind.

The wisest men are those who confess their poverty and ignorance in the secret corners of their hearts.

The unaware search for wisdom outside the reality of their own existence, thus distancing themselves from their truth.

Bearers carry unknown loads along the roads, boasting of that which they do not possess.

The wisdom of the wise does not give the power of creation to minds that do not hear.

Man will not succeed by garnering from windfalls; greed ruins the delicacy of the soul. Affection is dead in the dark soul of the covetous, and they like worms feed upon each other.

The odor of blood intoxicates their souls and they are brave in foul deeds.

The eyes of the greedy soon recognize the ways of cunning, and the moral law is twisted to their liking, infesting the purity of the soul.

Earthly substances drive the soul of man to baseness.

❖

The heavens invite the appointed,

The wild tulips and the water lilies,

The pure and transparent running water,

The song of the birds,

The glory of the setting and the rising sun and moon upon the horizon of the sea,

The splendor of the blossoms in spring,

The glittering of dew-drops upon the grass, and myriad other manifestations,

Are the tranquil melodies of the Gods that are hidden by nature's veils.

Oh, I wish that the pride of hearts would be shattered once again,

And truth would encompass the world,

And souls would shine like mirrors.

Until dawn the holy messengers whispered the realistic visions of the Gods upon the sky of existence,

And gave power to the life of man.

Believers have said that the last Psalm of the Gods which was uttered by the angels was:

In following rebellion and corruption's wake, the law of mercy is obstructed; trust in the Gods and wait, so that the streams of mercy flow in the land of the heart, and death reduces its hold.

And once again the tree of life blossoms and the messengers silently repeat the Psalm of the Gods in the sky of life.

Sadegh Angha
August 1963

Molana Shah Maghsoud Sadegh Angha, *"Pir Oveyssi"* has written well over 150 books, treatises, essays and other works on *Irfan* in prose and verse conveyed through different disciplines. These include:

	Written	Published
Psalm of the Gods	1955	1963
Iron	1950	1950
Principles of Faghr & Sufism	1974	1987
The Sufi Miracle — Commentary on the Holy Qur'an (11 volumes)	1962-1977*	
Owzan va Mizan (Weights and Balance)	1972	1973
Stages of Cognition in the Holy Qur'an	1972	1973
Manifestations of Thought	1950	1954
Message from the Soul	1960	1968
The Human Magnetic Body	1970	forthcoming
The Complete Arithmomancy	1967	forthcoming
Chanteh — Realm of the Sufi	1940	1943
Life	1970	forthcoming
Microbic Sages	1951	1951
Two Pulse Beats	1973	forthcoming
Remembrance	1965	forthcoming
Al-Salat	1978	1978
Purification & Enlightenment of Hearts	1978	1978
The Light of Salvation	1978	1978
The States of Enlightenment	1978	1978
The Hidden Angles of Life	1972	1974
Serr-ol Hajar	1960	1983
The Stages of the Seeker and the Ascent of Nader	1966	1983
The Mantle's Lineage	1945	1945
Through the Gates of the Unseen	1966	1983
The Traditional Medicine of Iran	1976	1978
Love and Fate	1938	1938
The Science of Numbers	1961	forthcoming
The Science of Names	1962	forthcoming
The Science of Coordinates and Squares	1962	forthcoming
The Principles of Oneness (The Epic of Life)	1966	1968
Ghazaliat	1960	1984
The Star in Literature	1931	1932
Kymya	1961	1972
Golzar-e Omid (The Flowers of Hope)	1963	1964
Nader's Treasure	(1940-1979)*	
The Rightful Visions	1970	forthcoming
Psalms of Truth	1962	1964
Nirvan	1955	1960
Heavenly Colors	1960	1984

*being compiled

Partial List of Works by the Author